SOUTHEAST
ALASKA

NANCY SIMMERMAN

FOREWORD BY JAMES A. MICHENER
TEXT BY SARAH EPPENBACH

GRAPHIC ARTS CENTER PUBLISHING COMPANY,
PORTLAND, OREGON

SOUTHEAST ALASKA

- - - - Alaska Marine Highway Routes
▲ Elevation in Feet

0 10 20 30 40 50 miles
0 10 20 30 40 50 kilometers

[SOUTHEAST ALASKA]

ISBN 0-932575-65-X
Library of Congress Catalog Number 88-80473
© MCMLXXXVIII by Graphic Arts Center Publishing Co.
Box 10306 • Portland, OR 97210 • 503/226-2402
Editor-in-Chief • Douglas A. Pfeiffer
Designer • Robert Reynolds
Cartographer • Thomas Patterson
Typographer • Harrison Typesetting, Inc.
Printer • Dynagraphics, Inc.
Bindery • Lincoln & Allen
Printed in the United States of America
Second Printing

■ *Frontispiece:* Nourished by abundant rainfall, moss carpets the spruce-hemlock forests of Southeast Alaska ■ *Right:* A silver thread of water cascades to a glacier-carved fjord.

■ *Left:* Stalks of Indian paintbrush brighten a salt chuck on a characteristically misty day. ■ *Above:* Due to the compact nature of the Southeast terrain, an astonishing variety of wildlife—from eagles to whales—coexists within the space of a few miles. These blue grouse dwell in the spruce-hemlock forest and in the alpine, building their nests on the ground.

■ *Above:* The rising spring sun warms the five hundred-mile Inside Passage, bathing the mountains in brilliant color. More than a thousand forested islands make up the Alexander Archipelago. Together with a narrow, mountainous strip of mainland adjoining British Columbia, they constitute Southeast Alaska, a dramatically contrasting landscape of mountains, glaciers, forests, and seas.

FOREWORD

by James A. Michener

Nancy Simmerman has built a distinguished career photographing her home state of Alaska in a way that captures its vast expanse, its grandeur, and its wonderful attractiveness to travelers who have never before experienced the far north. Visitors to Alaska have come to treasure Miss Simmerman's beautiful portraits of an unspoiled paradise and have gasped to see the stupendous qualities of some of the lesser known parts of the northland.

When I was working in her state, I profited constantly by referring to ALASKA II, to one or another of her pictures of places in which I was interested. Often, of course, I had seen the area myself, so her striking photographs were useful in refreshing my memory. But more often I realized that Miss Simmerman had lugged her camera into hidden corners that I would never have penetrated and was showing me aspects of the state I could not have found by myself.

From long study of her work I have concluded that she is first of all a young woman with the eye of an artist; she chooses her subjects well and photographs them exactly as they should be. This results in memorable pictures of much higher quality than you or I could achieve. Second, she must love to travel, for she gets into the most remote areas. Third, she is obviously an arduous worker, for merely to get to the sites recorded in her work required many days as well as much energy and money. This makes her work a major contribution, one that should survive for many years. Her photos constitute a valuable historical record.

Her emphasis in this book about Southeast Alaska is on a part of Alaska that I came to know intimately when I worked on a novel I had long planned. I lived in a log cabin on the campus of Sheldon Jackson College in the old Russian capital of Sitka and kept on my desk a form letter which I copied when writing to friends in the Lower 48 who inquired as to what life was like in frozen Alaska:

> The climate in Sitka is almost exactly like that in Philadelphia, except that up here we get less snow. Because the Japan Current sweeps past so close to shore, what snow does fall seems always to melt by noon. When I first arrived, my wife warned me, "Taking your daily walk here is not like taking one back in the States. Dress warmly!" I would cover myself in parkas and mufflers, but when I left my cabin and went out into the streets I found young people in shorts and T-shirts playing tennis or tossing a football, and I felt ridiculous.
>
> Then another phenomenon struck me. It was almost always wet outside, but the games went on and so did I. In fact, I never saw the streets of Sitka dry. I also never saw it rain. A lovely gray mist seemed to descend silently and invisibly; whereas Philadelphia's rainfall was about thirty-six inches a year, in Sitka it was closer to ninety-six.

The third phenomenon was an irritating one. Sitka, like most of the towns in southern Alaska, was surrounded by a rim of glorious mountains, making the area one of the most beautiful in the United States. The problem was they were visible about one day in forty, shrouded in impenetrable mists the rest of the time. Neighbors used to call us on the phone, "Hey! The mountains are out!" And there they would be, magnificently, for about forty-five minutes.

It is this compelling Alaska that Miss Simmerman has captured in this handsome book. She presents here the Alaska that summer visitors on their luxurious cruise ships see, the Alaska of glaciers, snow-covered mountains, great forests, and wonderful little towns perched on the edge of nowhere. I have long believed that the famous inland cruise leaving Vancouver and steaming up the Inside Passage to Southeast Alaska is one of the most rewarding in the world. For an endless unfolding of great scenery and mind-stimulating imagery, it is hard to beat.

A final word about Alaska, one that captivates me as I think of the happy times I've spent there. The top third of the state, north of the Arctic Circle, is an arctic desert with never a tree, no mountains, very little snow at any time, and literally thousands of shallow lakes which make the landscape from an airplane look as if it had a case of the measles. This book deals with a more bountiful part, the southern extremity that was discovered by Europeans and first settled by Indians and, later, Russians.

SOUTHEAST ALASKA is a colorful introduction to a massive state. We enjoy the area most when we bear in mind the other parts of Alaska that lie to the north. Each section of the state has its peculiar merit which it contributes to the greater mosaic.

JAMES A. MICHENER

SITKA, ALASKA

■ *Above:* With highway access to the "Outside" at only three points (Skagway, Haines, and Hyder), Southeast residents rely upon year-round ferry service for travel to Prince Rupert and Seattle as well as to neighboring towns. Although lacking some of the frills of luxury cruise ships, ferries offer private staterooms, viewing lounges, and dining service and carry automobiles as well as passengers. Here the ferry, *MV Columbia*, negotiates a narrow channel.

■ *Above:* "Flightseeing" by small plane or helicopter provides a thrilling look at such spectacular scenes as Big Goat Lake in Misty Fiords National Monument.
■ *Right:* Long and narrow like most Southeast communities, Ketchikan (population 14,300) clings to a ribbon of land between mountains and sea. A quarter of a million visitors—nearly four times the total population of Southeast Alaska—tour the Inside Passage in summer, the majority aboard luxury cruise ships.

■ *Left:* Seen from three thousand-foot Deer Mountain, Tongass Narrows separates the historic salmon cannery center of Ketchikan, on Revillagigedo Island, from the airport on Gravina Island. A small ferry shuttles passengers back and forth.
■ *Above:* Lights burn invitingly in the shops and galleries of Creek Street, where loggers and fishermen once shopped for bootleg whiskey and nighttime favors. In summer, salmon return to this creek to spawn.

■ *Above:* Tlingit Indian carver Nathan Jackson applies accent paint to a cedar totem at Saxman Totem Park outside of Ketchikan, one of several cultural centers where visitors can watch artists producing traditional Southeast Native crafts.
■ *Right:* Crafty Raven, crouched atop box, releases the sun into the firmament while the Old Man, his grandfather, looks on, in the Naa Kahidi Theater's dramatization of a Tlingit creation myth.

■ *Left:* Typical of Southeast topography, glacier-carved fjords extend deep into the granite-ledged mountains of Misty Fiords National Monument, accessible only by floatplane, helicopter, or boat. Eagles, bears, and mountain goats dwell here undisturbed. ■ *Above:* Replenished continually by rain and melting snow, streams cut through the coastal rain forest in their headlong rush to the sea.

■ *Above:* Evening quietude at Nooya Lake in 2.2 million-acre Misty Fiords National Monument reflects the serenity of the Southeast wilderness, a place of vast distances and few people. The high country abounds with tranquil lakes— some accessible by hike-in trails, others by floatplane or helicopter only. The Forest Service maintains more than one hundred sixty wilderness rental cabins in such magnificent waterfront settings, available for a very nominal fee.

LAND OF MOUNTAINS AND SEA

At 10:50 in the morning on Monday, March 30, 1987, Alaska Airlines flight #61 lifted off runway 26 at Juneau International Airport and climbed out to the northwest, bound for Yakutat. At about four hundred feet, the captain radioed that the airplane, a Boeing 737-200, had been struck by a fish. The fish, dropped by a startled bald eagle, hit the left side of the upper fuselage, causing a small dent and a two and one-half hour delay in Yakutat. The eagle flew away—hungry, but unharmed.

A bald eagle, a fish, and a jet plane. It's hard to imagine three more fitting symbols for the five hundred-mile strip of coastal mountains and offshore islands known as Southeast Alaska. Fifteen thousand bald eagles live along the rocky, forested shore of the Inside Passage. Five species of salmon spawn up the river drainages, and sixty-six thousand people depend upon jet airplanes for quick access to their remote and roadless realm.

The Southeast region of Alaska, also called the Panhandle, occupies the ribbon of land between Canadian British Columbia and the Pacific Ocean. The southern boundary falls at Dixon Entrance, the last stretch of unprotected water before entering Alaska's Inside Passage from the south. The northern limit extends to the colossal Malaspina Glacier near Yakutat.

The Southeast mainland is usurped by the Coast Mountains, the same mountain system that wraps around the Gulf of Alaska and onto the Aleutian chain. The mountains start modestly at the southern end of the Panhandle and increase in mass and height as they march northward, culminating in 18,008-foot Mount St. Elias at the juncture between the Panhandle and the rest of Alaska, or the handle and the pan.

The mountains drop abruptly into the Pacific Ocean, where they form more than a thousand tree-studded islands collectively called the Alexander Archipelago. The waterways of the Inside Passage thread between the islands and the coast like an intricate network of blood vessels, flooding the estuaries with nutrients and cleansing away the waste.

This dramatic marriage of mountains and sea dominates the landscape and provides a frame of reference for every aspect of life in Southeast Alaska. The glaciers flow between the mountains to the sea. The infant salmon swim down the rivers between the mountains and out to sea, and then return. The towns and villages turn their backs to the mountains and their eyes to the sea.

A resident of Ketchikan, Juneau, Haines, or Hoonah—of virtually any town or village—can hike to 2,000-foot alpine meadows in the morning and hook a salmon in the afternoon. The nearness of the forest and sea is a comfort zone of immeasurable importance. "I can leave my house and go to the end of the road—a five-minute walk—and get in my Lund and be on the water," says a friend who is a pilot, "or go sit by myself on an island."

People who live in Southeast feel an affinity for the land. The rhythms of the land reverberate through our bodies like a second heartbeat. We're tuned in to the cycles of nature. We know that in summer, for instance, the bears are feeding at the salmon streams and the deer up in the alpine. The whales are back. In fall, the Canada geese flock back to the wetlands. In winter, the bears den in the mountains and the deer come down on the beach. In spring, the king salmon migrate toward their spawning streams. We take pleasure in the signs of the seasons: the yellow shoots of skunk cabbage that herald spring, the magenta stalks of fireweed that measure summer's pace, the honking of the sandhill cranes passing overhead in fall.

The land is a partner that we turn to, at times for solace, at times for excitement, at times for sustenance in a literal way. In Southeast Alaska the land provides fish, game, and berries for the table and fuel for the stove. How much a household depends upon these resources is a function of location, culture, inclination, and economic necessity. I know hardly a family that doesn't go fishing or berrypicking on some occasion over the summer, primarily for recreation. Deer or moose hunting is less universal, but still prevalent.

Many households, even urban households, depend absolutely upon the land's bounty—the shelves of canned salmon and freezer packed with halibut and venison—to see them through the winter. In the outlying villages, an even greater proportion of people count on food gathering for subsistence. Recognizing this traditional dependency, the state of Alaska issues subsistence fishing permits which allow a limited amount of net fishing for salmon for personal consumption. For many older Alaska Natives, the habitual drive to harvest and store berries and salmon against the coming winter is both an emotional and an economic dependency. Out in the Bush, scores of rugged individualists practice a year-round subsistence life-style, a strenuous, never-ending routine of cutting firewood, catching and canning fish, putting up berries, pickling kelp, and gathering shells and seaweed to spread on the vegetable garden.

People who live in Southeast like to be outside. In summer, being outside means being on the water in anything that floats, from a kayak to a sailboat, or being in the mountains. Forest Service trails emanate from every town in Southeast Alaska. They wind through the heart of the spruce-hemlock forest and onto lofty ridges, which look down on interlocking waterways and across to ever more mountain peaks. In winter, when snow blankets the alpine and rivers freeze, snowshoes and skis come out. The hardy huddle in tents or cabins and fish through holes in the ice. Recreation tends toward the outdoors. Someone catches a salmon, and friends gather for a beach party. Blueberries ripen, and you pile kids and dogs in the car with a picnic lunch and make a day of it.

Living in the land of mountains and sea puts us in touch with nature. When I think of Southeast Alaska, I think of a bald eagle cruising low over the water, fishing; and a whale surfacing twenty yards from the skiff. I visualize the northern lights sweeping the sky on a clear, crisp September night. To me, living in Southeast means standing in a bower of evergreens, the moss soft beneath my feet; feeling the angry pull of salmon against monofilament; and anchoring in some gorgeous cove with no other humans in sight.

■ *Above:* The economy of Southeast Alaska revolves around the same extractive resources that have fueled the region since the purchase of Alaska from Russia in 1867: forest products, minerals, and seafood. Both canneries and cold storage processors operate in Southeast Alaska where clear, icy waters abound with salmon, halibut, shrimp, crab and several varieties of bottom fish. Colorful fishing boats jostle for space in the harbors of every community.

■ *Above:* Passengers visit aboard the *MV Columbia* while another Alaska ferry passes to stern. In summer, many travelers opt to sleep on the partially covered solarium deck, in lounge chairs, or in their tents. ■ *Right:* Fishing skiffs await action at Hydaburg, a Haida Indian village on Prince of Wales Island. Many Alaskans take advantage of state-sanctioned netting of salmon for subsistence purposes to gather the traditional winter food supply.

■ *Left:* Western hemlock, glowing in the sun, forms more than seventy percent of the coastal rainforest; Sitka spruce and cedar (the traditional wood for canoes and totem poles) make up most of the rest. ■ *Above:* Dressed in ceremonial button blankets, dancers from villages throughout Southeast Alaska steady a new totem pole at Saxman Totem Park, a symbol of the resurging pride in Native culture. ■ *Overleaf:* Pleasure craft, like these sailboats racing off Ketchikan, draw Southeasterners outdoors during foul weather as well as glorious days like this.

■ *Left:* Lovely, violet lupine—a "colonizing" plant that enriches the soil after glacial retreat—grows to four feet in height during the near twenty-four-hour daylight of summer. ■ *Above:* Yellow rain slickers hang outside cottages at Waterfall Resort, a former salmon cannery, on the west coast of Prince of Wales Island. Situated near prime salmon and halibut fishing grounds, fly-in wilderness lodges send visiting anglers home with pounds of packaged seafood.

■ *Above:* Alert eyes watch from the bridge as the ferry, *MV Malaspina*, slides through a shallow zig-zagging channel. Rushing tides, heavy traffic, and fog frequently complicate navigation. Wrangell Narrows, a constricted, twenty-one-mile passage between Mitkof and Kupreanof islands that contains more than seventy navigational markers, and Peril Strait, a diagonal cut between Baranof and Chichagof islands, demand especially close attention.

ISLAND EXISTENCE

Not every community in Southeast Alaska is located on an island, but most are, or might as well be. Juneau lies on the mainland, though you can't drive anywhere from there. Like Ketchikan, Wrangell, and Petersburg (like every community, in fact, except Skagway, Haines, and Hyder), the state capital can be reached only by air or by water—a matter of excruciating frustration to residents of Southcentral Alaska, who number more than half of the state's population.

Despite the difficulties of access, isolation accounts for much of Southeast Alaska's charm. Our highways, for instance, are made of water. Every season of the year, the fjords and channels that connect Southeast Alaska towns reverberate with the engines of ships moving people and cargo along the "marine highway" from Seattle to Yakutat. Brightly painted tugboats shepherd rafts of logs to waiting cargo ships and mills. Barges piled high with all manner of goods, from mobile homes to cabin cruisers, leave Seattle once a week for ports that asphalt highways never reach.

In summer, magnificent cruise ships, sleek as pampered kittens, promenade the length of the Inside Passage. The grandest among them house more people than live in many of the towns along their route. The ships are islands unto themselves. The generators aboard the largest, which carry twenty-two-hundred passengers, for instance, could easily power the city of Ketchikan.

The big, blue-hulled ferries of the Alaska Marine Highway System carry everything from circus animals to high school swim teams. Like dependable draft horses, they plow up and down the archipelago, stopping at each town in turn. When they reach Skagway, the northernmost ferry port, they reverse the process heading south, day in and day out, irrespective of holidays or weather. Smaller ferries travel to and from the farthest-flung outposts of Southeast Alaska—villages like Angoon and Kake and fishing towns like Pelican. At times, entire communities seem to be aboard: mothers with children in tow on their way to shop in Ketchikan or Juneau, fishermen going home or returning to their boats, loggers coming and going from camp.

Other than the predictable delays in loading and off-loading, about the only things that hold up a ferry are the tide going through Wrangell Narrows and Peril Strait, and fishermen. I have ridden the ferry when the gill net vessels were clustered so thickly on Lynn Canal outside of Haines that threading a path between them was like negotiating traffic in Manhattan. Weather holds no sway. Few sights upon this earth can be as heartwarming as an Alaska ferry, tied up at some lonely terminal on a snowy winter night, with every light blazing.

Where the ferries won't take you, bush planes will. Fitted with wheels or floats (sometimes both), they buzz like dragonflies through mountain passes and follow valleys down to the sea, depositing passengers at isolated lodges or remote communities like Elfin Cove, way up north on Chichagof Island. They deliver mail and swoop down to leave off or pick up fishermen at wilderness lakes. Southeast residents display a singular ease around boats and little planes—one mark of an insular existence. Children in Southeast Alaska grow up discussing Cessnas and Beavers the way generations of Lower 48 drivers have bandied about Chevies and Fords. Not a few Southeasterners could pilot a plane before they knew how to operate a car.

Where floatplanes can't go, helicopters can. Capable of landing virtually anywhere, from the tiniest pocket of alpine meadow to the slimmest moon of beach, they deposit geologists and tourists onto glaciers; help wildlife biologists count bears or mountain goats; and ferry photographers, prospectors, and a host of other people and equipment into otherwise inaccessible locations.

Among the ferries, jet planes, air taxis, and boats in Southeast, roads are hardly missed. People are constantly on the move. In many respects, Southeast Alaska feels like one big neighborhood strung out over five hundred miles. If you lived in Los Angeles, it would be unusual to run into someone you knew in Bakersfield, a hundred miles away. In Southeast Alaska, a community a hundred miles away is just next door, the next stop on the ferry line. Every airport on the Panhandle is a meeting place for old friends and business acquaintances.

On islands, the sense of community is very strong. Strangers help each other out. "Thank you to all the people who stopped and asked if they could help me when I had vehicle trouble on the Thorne Bay road on Thursday, July 16th," reads a letter to the editor in the *Prince of Wales Island News*. "Your help and offers of help were much appreciated." In Yakutat, where a local bumper sticker claims that "Outsiders Never Wave," drivers signal greetings to every fellow motorist. In this great and, at times, forbidding land, we know our neighbors personally—not just by name—and depend upon them. Friendships run deep (animosities, too).

Island living makes people self-reliant emotionally as well as physically. Most entertainment must be invented, an activity that Southeasterners approach with unbridled enthusiasm. Parades, carnivals, and contests draw enthusiastic crowds regardless of season or weather. A summer poster reminds Petersburg townspeople of an upcoming Wonderfulness Parade ("Humans, dogs, slow-moving vehicles— more fun than a good tickle"). A group of capital city residents helicopter a piano to the top of 3,800-foot Mount Roberts, one of the two big mountains that rear up behind Juneau, for a summer solstice party with attire "formal or none at all." In Skagway, cheering fans mass to hear the Bigger Hammer Marching Band, whose instruments consist of kazoos masquerading as tubas and trombones (made of cardboard and spray-painted gold).

The vicissitudes of an island existence dictate a certain nonchalance in matters outside of our control. When winter storms make a mockery of airline schedules, we may not leave on vacation after all. A concert might unexpectedly lack the guest soloist from the Lower 48. At its most trying, life in Southeast Alaska takes on a distinctly comic air. Government employees board a southbound jet in Anchorage on their way to the capital for a meeting; overfly fogbound Juneau and end up in Sitka, Ketchikan, or Seattle; then board another jet going north; overfly Juneau again; and land back where they started. My husband once shuttled between Anchorage and Seattle for four days, trying to get home to Juneau.

■ *Above:* A fisherman readies his boat for another season in Craig, a lumber and fishing town on Prince of Wales Island, reached by ferry from Ketchikan.
■ *Overleaf:* Established by the Alaska Native Claims Settlement Act of 1971, Native village and regional corporations invested heavily in timber operations, such as this log sort yard in the Tlingit Indian village of Klawock.

■ *Above:* Dressed in gold rush finery, the "Shady Ladies" wave a cruise ship into Wrangell (population 2,400) on the northern tip of Wrangell Island, where prospectors paused on their way to the Canadian interior. ■ *Right:* Tangy crimson and orange salmonberries grow extravagantly throughout Southeast Alaska. Along with blueberries, they are gathered for pies, jellies, and freezer. ■ *Overleaf:* The sun glints over a timeless scene of mountains, sea, and kelp.

■ *Left:* Water plunges over moss-covered rocks, seeking a route to the sea. Winter will transform the scene into a glittering icefall between snow-covered banks. ■ *Above:* Fern-covered stumps show where old-growth forest once was logged. Smaller, evenly-spaced trees have grown into the clearing. ■ *Overleaf:* Indian paintbrush glows with color at Blind Slough near Petersburg, one of the northernmost wintering areas for trumpeter swans.

■ *Left:* A Coast Guard crew tends a critical solar-powered navigation light. Such aids to navigation guide helmsmen through the maze of rocks, islands, and narrow passageways that make up the Inside Passage. ■ *Above:* New Eddystone Rock, an ancient volcanic plug, occupies a lonely island in Misty Fiords.

■ *Above:* Norwegian descendants of Petersburg's first settlers celebrate their heritage during the annual Little Norway Festival in May. The young woman on the left models the specially designed Petersburg *bunad*, embroidered with Southeast wildflowers, which every Petersburg woman—of Norwegian ancestry or not—is entitled to wear. Nearly every town in Southeast hosts an annual festival in celebration of a unique heritage or event.

TO FISH FOR A LIVING

My friend Eric McDowell started fishing from a beach cabin near Juneau when he was seven. He spent a lot of time alone and pulled in halibut after halibut. Then, in college, working in a Petersburg cannery one summer, he signed on with a halibut boat that was short a crew member. When the season ended, he asked the skipper if he could stay on and fish tuna over the winter. The skipper said if Eric had a place waiting for him at college, he ought to go back to school. The skipper said his crew was full of men who had been fishing for twenty years because they didn't know how to do anything else, and it really wasn't a very nice life.

So Eric finished college and graduate school, and started a consulting business in Juneau. But pretty soon he bought a little troller, and about May of every year, when the snow flurries stopped blowing across Gastineau Channel and the alders unfurled their tender leaves, he would begin slipping out of the office and down to the harbor to work on the boat. While the Legislative session dragged wearily to its June conclusion, tying him to the capital, his mind would be on the boats tacking out in the Fairweather Grounds on the outside coast. One day the southwesterlies would blow in from the ocean and the town would taste of the sea, or the morning would dawn crisp and cloudless and the Chilkat Range would be stretched out against the sky like a big hand beckoning, and Eric would be gone to catch the fleet.

In spring, life begins anew for commercial fishermen in Southeast Alaska. Down to the docks they stream, in knitted watch caps and heavy woolen halibut shirts, carrying blow torches and sandpaper, tool kits and cases of paper towels, bottom paint and diesel oil. They strip off the visqueen, crack open the hatch, mop up the moisture, replace the oil filter, and baby the engine back to life. Then they put the boat up on the ways, check the through-hull fittings, scrape the barnacles and seaweed off the bottom, and slap on a coat of paint. A newborn foal in Kentucky doesn't kindle as much innocent hope as a fishing boat in spring. Maybe this will be the season. Maybe the fish will be there this year.

The rest of us, the non-fishermen, watch them getting ready with ill-disguised longing. Theirs is a world we glimpse but never see. Oh, we stand shoulder to shoulder with them at counters of countless marine supply stores. While they buy spare gaskets and replacement floats, we ask shyly how the season's going and speculate on the weather. But we don't kid ourselves about being in any way like them. There are only four kinds of *real* Alaskan after all: loggers, prospectors, bush pilots, and fishermen. Out on the water, trolling for salmon from our sportfishing boats, we eavesdrop on their radio conversations, hungering for knowledge. In far-off harbors like Craig, where the big seiners wait for the next opening, we feel the tension mount and wonder what it's like out there.

Fishing is a sensory experience, Eric says. You go by the feel of things. The way the boat rides the swells. The color of the sky. How the wind sounds in the rigging. (Is it higher pitched than it was ten minutes ago? Should you cut your gear and run?) You have a sensation of wholeness—the wind, the rain, the sea, the fish, the boat, the hum of the engine. When things are going well, you're in tune with what's going on down in the water. You *know* when a fish is going to strike.

Eric: "One of my favorite things is anchoring in some natural harbor on the coast in real rugged weather. I can feel the wind move the boat at anchor, and I'm warm inside. There are a million places to anchor up, and they're all special . . . and everybody out there feels the same way I do."

Eric says the worst thing about fishing is "being regulated—told when and where you can fish and what you can and can't catch."

There was a time when the fisheries weren't regulated at all. Canneries operated twenty-four hours a day and the salmon stocks were depleted. Fish traps were outlawed at the time of statehood (except at Metlakatla, the Tsimshian Indian reservation on Annette Island). The next step to rebuilding the fish stocks was to limit the fishermen.

At the start of the 1970s, if you wanted to troll for king salmon, which are the money fish, you paid $35 for the necessary commercial licenses and bought a boat. The trolling season opened on the outer coast April 15, and from then until October 31—over six months—you could fish day-round. The inside waters never closed. In 1975, Alaska initiated the Limited Entry program to reduce the amount of gear fishing in Alaska waters. Then, the Alaska Department of Fish and Game increasingly regulated the time and place fishermen could fish, juggling openings to allow sufficient escapement up spawning streams and to honor various multi-state and international fishery treaties.

Today the movements of all the major fleets that fish the waters of Southeast Alaska—the trollers, gill-netters, seiners that harvest salmon, and the longliners fishing for halibut—are orchestrated by news releases and broadcasts from the Commercial Fisheries Division of the Alaska Department of Fish and Game. If you want to troll for king salmon, you first have to acquire a power troll entry permit, which sells on the open market for around $27,000. Then you have to wait for Fish and Game to tell you when and where to fish. In the 1987 season, the king salmon troll fishery was open a total of twenty-four days, except for some spot closures in outside waters. The gill net fleet fished a series of one- to five-day openings. The longest purse seine openings lasted thirty-nine hours.

The young people starting out can put up with the regulations. They've never experienced wide-open commercial fishing. The older fishermen don't have a choice. Like the skipper said, they don't know how to work at anything else. Some of the rest have faced a hard decision.

"I love fishing," Eric says. "All my relatives are Icelandic cod fishermen, and I honestly believe there is some sort of hereditary disposition toward the sea. If the troll fishery had remained unregulated, I would still be a commercial fisherman today."

Stilt houses reflect in Hammer's Slough, a saltwater inlet that bisects the town of Petersburg.

51

■ *Previous Page:* An iceberg from Shakes Glacier, which terminates in a tributary of the Stikine River, dwarfs this Wrangell excursion boat. ■ *Left:* Proud couple exhibits the prize-winning forty-eight-pound, three-ounce king salmon they captured during a fishing derby. ■ *Above:* Totem poles rise like sentries from Shakes Island in Wrangell Harbor, once occupied by Stikine Tlingit Indians. The hand-adzed Bear Tribal House replicates a traditional Tlingit clan house.

■ *Above:* Anchored along the shore of many communities and in isolated coves and inlets, float houses ride gently on the tide and settle onto mud flats when the water recedes. ■ *Right:* The setting sun washes the blue-green landscape of the Inside Passage with shimmering orange and gold. Persistent low-hanging mists make such elaborate displays a rarity in Southeast Alaska.

■ *Left:* Summer wildflowers, like this bay laurel, brighten beaches and alpine meadows. ■ *Above:* Humpback whales migrate from breeding grounds in Mexico or Hawaii to summer in Alaska. Here one "sounds," or dives, near Prince of Wales Island. ■ *Overleaf:* Devil's Thumb Mountain forms an impressive backdrop to Petersburg (population 3,300) on Mitkof Island. Norwegian Peter Buschmann chose this spot for the fish processing town because of abundant salmon and halibut and a ready supply of ice from nearby LeConte Glacier.

■ *Above:* Intertidal life thrives in the cold, clear waters of Kootznahoo Inlet near Angoon on Admiralty Island, where strong currents constantly replenish the food supply. ■ *Right:* An uprooted tree on the Stikine River delta attests to the power of this international waterway that flows unhindered for three hundred thirty miles. A historic trade route between Indians of the interior and the coast, the Stikine later carried thousands of prospectors to Canadian goldfields.

■ *Left:* A cruise ship noses into twenty-five-mile Tracy Arm, south of Juneau. Such narrow, steep-walled fjords, some as deep as four hundred feet, were carved by advancing glaciers thousands of years ago. The sea flooded in as the ice retreated.
■ *Above:* A winter sun, reflected in the still waters of Auke Lake, kisses the Mendenhall Towers while Mendenhall Glacier slumbers in shadow.

■ *Above:* Stan Price hauls firewood to his cabin near a salmon stream where brown bears congregate to feed on Admiralty Island. He has gained national renown during his long and peaceful stay among the bruins. ■ *Right:* New growth on this western hemlock heralds the arrival of spring. Within the space of a few weeks, lingering drifts of snow recede and the landscape erupts in a frenzy of green, an eagerly awaited event known as "greening up."

Steller's sea lions watch a handcrafted skiff glide along Tenakee Inlet on Chichagof Island.

WILDLIFE

Along the short road from the ferry terminal to the village of Angoon on Admiralty Island, a clearing in the trees overlooks Kootznahoo Inlet. One day I glanced over the side of the road at this clearing and saw a flash of silver in the water; a huge school of herring were performing a water ballet. At the same place the next day, a pair of harbor porpoises nosed along the shore. The third time I paused in that magic spot, a bald eagle burst into view like a conjurer's pigeon and settled heavily into a hemlock tree not ten feet away.

In Southeast Alaska, brown bears and black bears, moose, deer, mountain goats, humpback whales and orca, porpoises, sea lions, eagles, salmon, halibut, and countless other creatures coexist within the space of a few miles. Only the volume of wildlife surpasses the variety: not an eagle or two, but, at the right time of year, *thirty-five hundred* of them, all in one place. In summer, the pink salmon lie so thick at the entrance to the spawning streams that their humped backs protruding from the water look like a path of shiny black cobblestones stretching into the distance. Seeing these wild creatures in their natural habitat—tuning into their patterns and watching for their appearance as the seasons turn—is one of the greatest pleasures of living in Southeast Alaska.

In summer, humpback whales return from their wintering grounds in Mexico and Hawaii to feed in the krill-rich bays and inlets of the Inside Passage. You see them in places like Frederick Sound and Glacier Bay. First the telltale waterspout appears, then the glistening back that arches in slow motion, followed by the huge lobed tail.

Lying by a campfire on the beach at night or drifting at anchor in a silent cove, you sometimes hear a whooshing of air way out on the water—the sound of the great whales, breathing.

Orca, or killer whales, the black-and-white "wolves of the sea," generate a flutter of excitement wherever they roam. They travel in packs, fast, their tall dorsal fins slicing through the water at speeds of twenty-five knots and more. Dall and harbor porpoise are more fun, hurrying over to play chicken with passing boats. May signals the start of the breeding season at the sea lion rookery on Benjamin Island, at the entrance to Lynn Canal north of Juneau. Alaska state ferries pass right by on the way to Haines and Skagway.

Both brown bears (grizzlies) and black bears live in Southeast. Admiralty Island, called "Kootznahoo" or "fortress of the bears" in the Tlingit language, contains what is probably the highest concentration of brown bears in the world: approximately one bear for every one of the island's 1,700 square miles. (Other brown bear habitats include parts of the mainland and the northernmost islands.) Admiralty has been a bear island for a very long time. From the air you can see oval depressions on the alpine ridges where generations of brown bears have planted their feet, year after year, for perhaps ten thousand years. The Admiralty bears den on the mountain slopes in winter and emerge in spring to feed on berries. As summer progresses, they descend to congregate at salmon streams.

Black bears inhabit the mainland and the southern islands of Southeast. Like their larger cousins, they eat both berries and salmon. I have seen black bears in the forest and in the mountains only rarely and always at a distance, but in Juneau I have seen black bears—garbage bears—on my stairs, in my yard, under the porch of my house in town. No matter how civilized Alaska cities may appear, they are only a toehold in the wilderness.

The delicate Sitka black-tailed deer move opposite the bears, migrating to the high alpine in summer and coming down in winter to shelter and browse under the forest canopy or, if winter is severe, forage on the beach. Higher up, long-haired mountain goats clamber over the rocky shoulders of the mountains on their special spongy hooves, not much concerned with the doings of people far below. Seen from the air, their white coats stand out sharply against the green meadows. Moose wander the banks and gravel bars of several rivers, nibbling the tender willow shoots. The largest herd roams near Yakutat at the northern end of the Panhandle.

Before the snow leaves the ground, rufous hummingbirds arrive in Southeast gardens from their winter in Mexico, impatient for the bright blossoms of spring. Canada geese show up then, too, and feed upon the succulent marshlands. All through the year, jet black ravens wing through the dripping conifer forests, as comical and mysterious today as they appeared to the first inhabitants along these coasts. On windy days they tumble and slide down the airstreams high overhead, the envy of earthbound observers.

In summer, bald eagles are as familiar as sparrows most everywhere in Southeast. From late October through January, as many as thirty-five hundred of them move to the Chilkat River near Haines, where warm water springs entice a late run of chum salmon. The eagles cluster in the cottonwood trees along the river, in full view of cars passing along the Haines Highway. The shoreline of Admiralty Island supports some nine hundred bald eagle nests. The adult eagles, colored brown with white heads, raise one or two brown-and-white chicks in their massive nests. The young birds retain their mottled coloring until their third or fourth year.

Alaska used to pay bounty for eagles. From 1917 to 1952, hunters killed an estimated one hundred twenty-nine thousand bald eagles for fifty cents apiece (later two dollars) because the government considered them a threat to spawning salmon and fox farms, an industry that flourished during the 1920s and 1930s and then evaporated. Now protected, bald eagles currently number ten to fifteen thousand in Southeast Alaska; their greatest threat comes not from guns but from destruction of their habitat. No matter how long you live in Southeast, seeing these lords of the sky—wings outstretched to seven feet, white heads glistening, angry yellow eyes staring down the whole world—remains the most precious of gifts. Like the bears, the whales, and the Canada geese that flock upon the wetlands, they favor us with their presence. We notice when they go away and watch for their return.

■ *Previous Page:* Fragile shooting stars provide pockets of color in a field of green. ■ *Left:* A white scar traces an avalanche chute in Tracy Arm fjord. The icebergs sheared from the face of a nearby glacier. ■ *Above:* Sawyer Glacier litters Tracy Arm with myriad tiny icebergs. The juxtaposition of mountains, forest, glacier, and sea typifies the landscape of Southeast Alaska.

■ *Above:* A brown bear sow and cub move with amazing ease along the sheer cliffs of this glacial fjord. Known also as grizzlies, brown bears inhabit the mainland and northern islands of the Inside Passage and feed on spawning salmon. ■ *Right:* Passengers on the deck of Alaska ferries, such as the *MV Taku,* enjoy the view of mountains and even occasional wildlife. ■ *Overleaf:* These Steller's sea lions will soon leave their winter rookery to follow a spring herring run.

■ *Left:* Delicate Sitka black-tailed deer weigh only one hundred to one hundred fifty pounds. ■ *Above:* Humpback, or pink, salmon migrating up Anan Creek, south of Wrangell, attract black bears in the spring. An observatory allows for cautious viewing. Much smaller than grizzlies, black bears are at home on the mainland and on most of the islands in Southeast.

■ *Above:* A lone float house bobs serenely on Gastineau Channel near Juneau.
■ *Right:* "Termination dust"—signaling time for prospectors to come out of the hills—powders thirty-six hundred-foot Mount Juneau behind the state capital. Founded in 1880 by the discovery of gold-bearing ore, Juneau (population 29,400) once housed the largest gold milling operation in the world. The city now depends on government to employ one of every two workers.

■ *Left:* Wickersham State Historic Site, Juneau home of U.S. District Judge James Wickersham, brings Southeast's rich history into focus. ■ *Above:* Welcome July sunshine entices Juneau office workers to Marine Park's waterfront setting. ■ *Overleaf:* The twelve-mile Mendenhall Glacier, accessible by car, flows out of the fifteen hundred-square-mile Juneau Ice Field. Rocks and dirt that have fallen from valley walls darken the tortured surface.

On a bleak Juneau day, a lunch stand awaits business in front of the 1930s-era state capitol.

FOREST IN TRANSITION

We meet at the Temsco Heliport in Juneau on a soft summer morning, an all-too-rare phenomenon in cool, drizzly Southeast Alaska. The helicopter, a five-passenger A-Star, strains at the bit, rotors fanning. Bob Engelbrecht, our pilot, swings into the cockpit. We fasten seatbelts, clamp on headsets that let us talk over the rhythmic fwap-fwap-fwap of the blades, and head out to look at glaciers.

There's no great trick to finding them in this northern part of the Panhandle; the mountains literally drip with glaciers. They roll out of hidden ice fields, ancient, luminous highways of ice, battering their way to the sea. The Mendenhall, a Mississippi River sort of glacier, spills downward for twelve miles. In its expanse, the glacier is like a desert, but no desert ever had such motion or hinted at such secrets. The ice undulates in all directions, smooth except at the edges, where the glacier accordions back on itself in gigantic slabs and building blocks. House-sized boulders, fallen from adjoining cliffs years or decades past, repose upon the glacier, marooned, now, for the long ride down.

We fly up the Mendenhall to its source and look down upon a vast white plain. Fifteen hundred square miles of ice and snow stretch into the horizon, broken only by nunataks, pyramids of rock that project above the snow. Forty major glaciers and over a hundred small ones surge to life here in the Juneau Ice Field, fed by copious quantities of compacted snow. The earth below is totally white—not the white of a winter snowfall that cloaks the garden until the greening of spring, but the fathomless white of a landscape that has never known color and never will.

Minutes later we are back at sea level, inspecting emerald estuaries that sustain thousands of migrating seabirds and angling over the tip of Douglas Island. Around the perimeter, the rain forest spreads her mossy skirts to the water's edge. Our route now lies higher, above the dense thicket of hemlock and spruce, where deer and mountain goats grow fat in summer. We land beside a quiet lake and step into the pastel landscape of the alpine: the misty blue of lupine and blueberries, the delicate pink of shooting stars, the silver of wind-sculpted bark.

All this—glaciers, ice fields, forest, islands, alpine meadows—falls within the Tongass National Forest. Established in 1907, the nation's largest national forest encompasses virtually all of the land mass of Southeast Alaska, 16.8 million acres in all (three times the size of Massachusetts). The Tongass contains old growth rain forest—miles and miles of which have never even been seen—hurtling rivers, and mountain lakes that have yet to be named. Forest rangers who have worked both in Alaska and the Lower 48 say that even the areas of the Tongass that are classified as conventional national forest contain more true wilderness than any of the designated wilderness sites down south.

The forest is vast; people are few. Anyone who has hiked a national forest trail in the Lower 48 is stupefied by the low human impact on trails in the Tongass. You can hike the most popular trail in Southeast Alaska on the finest day in summer and probably encounter fewer people than you would on the first quarter-mile of a trail down south. The Tongass encompasses 5.5 million acres of designated wilderness, including Admiralty Island National Monument, which counts two eagle nests for every mile of shoreline, and Misty Fiords National Monument, a 2.2 million-acre refuge of primeval fjords bounded by three-thousand-foot cliffs. But not even the Tongass is big enough to accommodate the increasing demands of people.

As the resident and visitor populations expand in Southeast Alaska, the pressure on the forest grows in step. Timber and mineral production, tourism, wildlife and fishery enhancement, hiking, camping, fishing, hunting, and boating compete for the forest resources. Unfortunately, many of these activities clash. Timber harvest and mining create jobs and build roads, but also endanger salmon streams and wildlife habitat and leave behind unsightly scars. Recreational trails open up the wilderness, but impinge upon delicate plant life. Helicopters and airplanes provide access to locales that most people would never see, enhancing tourism, but pollute the environment with noise and fumes.

The Tongass is a forest in transition. The growing pains are acute. The intense controversy over logging in the Tongass involves not simply trees, but people. Politicians, fishermen, environmentalists, mill operators, Forest Service employees—all have a stake in the issue. Most concerned of all, of course, are the loggers.

Everything about the loggers' life-style serves to distance them from the rest of the population. They live apart in their own communities, talk their own lingo, wear their own brand of uniform, even write their own genre of poetry. Like fishermen, they represent the Alaska that Juneau office workers can only wonder about. Today they are an endangered species, victims of a complex world in which everything that was right to do for half a century now seems to be totally wrong.

Richard Gildersleeve, a big bear of a man with a gentle voice, is the very image of an Alaskan logger. A third-generation float camp logger, he is boss of the Gildersleeve logging camp at Polk Inlet on Prince of Wales Island. He has lived in logging camps all his life and he wouldn't live anyplace else. He could fly a plane practically before he could walk. It pains him that there is a road, albeit one fraught with obstacles, into his camp. He prefers isolation, the traditional lot of float camp life.

You need only about three minutes with Richard Gildersleeve to feel his love for the forest and the logging life. "When you're in really nice logs and really nice deflection, and the weather's good, everything is just like playing," he says. "The better things go, the better everybody's spirits are, and it just gets to be great. . . . I wouldn't trade living in Southeast for anything. I just enjoy the country so much."

■ *Above:* The Juneau International Airport sprawls over the valley carved by the mile-wide Mendenhall Glacier, which has retreated two and one-half miles in the past two hundred thirty years. With few roads to the "Outside," Southeast residents rely heavily upon scheduled air service, which includes float planes and wheeled Bush aircraft as well as commercial jet planes.

■ *Above:* Skiers seek untrodden slopes above the highest chairlift at Eaglecrest Ski Area on Douglas Island, a short drive from Juneau. ■ *Right:* Helicopters whisk visitors to a guided walk on the hauntingly beautiful moonscape of Mendenhall Glacier. ■ *Overleaf:* Viewed from a snow-sculpted vista on Douglas Island, mountains and sea stretch into the horizon in an endlessly repeating pattern.

■ *Left:* Port of call at Juneau, as in other cities and towns, allows time to wander the streets, visit the shops and restaurants, and take in the culture. Although the City and Borough of Juneau has thirty-one hundred square miles, one of the nation's largest communities in area, the highway extends only forty miles. ■ *Above:* Spraying foam refreshes float trip passengers on the Mendenhall River.

■ *Above:* Winter wears many faces in coastal Southeast. Here a sunset fog shrouds the Mendenhall wetlands in mystery. Although the temperature rarely falls below zero, daylight plummets from some eighteen hours on the longest day in summer to six or seven hours at winter solstice. ■ *Right:* A red channel marker competes gamely against the gaudy light of the setting moon.

■ *Left:* The sixty-six thousand residents of Southeast are concentrated in seven major towns and several smaller communities. Between them stretch peopleless panoramas of mountains, islands, and sea. ■ *Above:* "Liquid sunshine" sparkles in the cupped leaves of lupine. An average one hundred inches of annual precipitation keeps forests green and lush, fills salmon-spawning streams, and feeds glaciers with fresh loads of snow. ■ *Overleaf:* Mount Edgecumbe, an extinct volcano visible from Sitka, rises Fuji-like from Kruzof Island.

■ *Left:* With the sun just topping the mountains on Sitka Sound, a lone troller heads out to the fishing grounds. When fishing, the outriggers, now fastened in the vertical position, extend horizontally over the water, trailing multiple lines with baited hooks. Troll-caught king or coho—immediately removed from the line, killed, cleaned, and iced—bring the highest price of any salmon. ■ *Above:* Cruise ships anchor off Sitka while their passengers visit ashore.

■ *Above:* Largest boats in the Southeast fleet, purse seiners require a crew of six. Here the seine crew hauls in the net in choppy water off Dall Island on the outer coast. To make the set, a powerful skiff draws the net outward in an arc from the seine boat. ■ *Right:* The seine-caught salmon will be iced and stored in the hold until they can be off-loaded to a cannery tender or dock for processing.

■ *Left:* Hearty youngsters brave the harbor waters at Pelican. A boardwalk fishing and cannery village on the northwest tip of Chichagof Island, Pelican hums with activity in summer and quiets in winter. ■ *Above:* Southeast Alaska's ten thousand miles of shoreline, ten million acres of forest, and some one thousand islands form an intricate jigsaw puzzle. In such limitless wilderness, the lazy drone of a small airplane can sound welcome indeed.

■ *Above:* The whirling New Archangel Dancers pay tribute to Sitka's historic role as the capital of Russian America and enthrall audiences with their colorful folk dances from the old country. ■ *Right:* Fog softly drapes the inner harbor of Elfin Cove on north Chichagof Island, where commercial trollers lay over between trips to the nearby Fairweather fishing grounds. Roadless, airportless, and ferry-less, Elfin Cove retains the charm of isolation.

A totem pole watches from Sitka National Historical Park, where Russians battled Tlingit Indians in 1804.

FIRST PEOPLE

According to legends, ancestors of the coastal Indians of Southeast Alaska followed the river valleys out of Interior Canada until they reached the sea. The Tlingit, the "People of the Tide," settled in villages along a five hundred-mile stretch of coast and islands between Yakutat Bay and the Portland Canal, now the southern boundary of Alaska. The Haida established themselves to the south, on the coast of British Columbia and the Queen Charlotte Islands. In the late 17th or early 18th century, they extended their range northward and claimed the southern end of Prince of Wales Island in Alaska. The third Southeast Native group, the Tsimshian, lived along the Nass and Skeena rivers in British Columbia. In 1887, a missionary led a group of Tsimshian to Annette Island near Ketchikan, where they founded the village of Metlakatla and the Annette Island Indian Reserve.

The early Southeast Natives lived in cedar longhouses that they built along riverbanks or protected coves or inlets, facing the sea. Their immediate surroundings yielded materials to satisfy most of their needs. From the sea they obtained plentiful salmon, halibut, seaweed, and shellfish. The forest provided summer berries that, like salmon, could be preserved for winter; wood for heat and shelter; tree roots and bark for weaving, cooking, and storage baskets; and stout canoes to carry them on hunting, trading, social, and warring missions the length of their island chain and beyond.

The abundant resources of their misty land resulted in a culture that was wealthy both in leisure time and material goods. Their highly developed sense of style manifested itself in virtually every object, from the humblest wooden halibut hook to intricately woven baskets of spruce roots and cedar bark, carved wooden feast dishes, and dazzling Chilkat blankets made of mountain goat hair twined with cedar bark. Out of this heritage, too, came the cedar totem poles carved to honor an individual, family or clan or signify an important event, such as a potlatch. The poles traditionally were left to weather peacefully, their sparse natural dyes fading year by year while the moss crept stealthily into cracks formed by sun and rain. Some of the old poles have since been roused from sleep in abandoned villages and brought back to museums. Others, reclaimed by the forest from which they sprang, still keep their secrets of the past.

Like the Eskimos, Aleuts, and Athapaskans of northern, western, and interior Alaska, Southeast Natives balance gingerly between the world their ancestors knew and a world defined by corporate identities and high tech communications. Instead of sharing space in a clan house, they share stock in village and regional corporations. The refreshments at a modern-day potlatch—likely to take place at folding tables in a community hall—include both traditional and convenience foods, from smoked salmon and herring roe on kelp to frozen pizza and packaged sheet cakes. The Native sitting next to you on the jet from Seattle might be returning to a simple frame house in a village with dirt streets or a high rise condominium in a city center, and might work in a high-paying corporate or government job or fish for a living.

While increasingly camouflaged by contemporary trappings, aspects of the traditional culture remain strong. New totem poles stand proudly in many towns and villages. A new generation of basket and blanket weavers struggles to keep these difficult art forms alive. Indian dance groups enjoy enthusiastic support. To see teenagers performing the old dances, their button blankets rippling over faded blue jeans and running shoes, is to glimpse a culture that is thriving, even if the ancient languages are heard but rarely.

The dichotomy between old and new ways is most apparent in the lives of the Elders, whose English may be broken or non-existent. When the fullness of summer brings the salmon to the head of the streams and the blueberries bulge with juice, Native women leave their modern apartments, their dishwashers, and their central heating. They file into the woods, just as their mothers and grandmothers did before them, to pick berries for winter. The salmon must be smoked and canned. If you traveled to Sitka in early spring, you would see Native people placing hemlock boughs in the bay for the herring to spawn upon, then collecting them again, heavy with roe, for drying or freezing. If you made your way to the Chilkat River near Haines, you could watch them netting the smelt-like eulachon fish and rendering them for their vitamin-rich oil.

For the old ones, the land of forest and sea remains a marvelous and somewhat mysterious world in which man occupied a humbler place. When Steve Brown and Richard Dalton prepared to carve a traditional Tlingit hunting canoe at Glacier Bay National Park, 90-year-old George Dalton, Sr., of Hoonah (Richard's father)—the inspiration for the project and very likely the last person to have participated in building such a canoe—was uneasy because the appropriate ceremonies had not taken place. The old way of his people would have been to speak to the canoe tree before felling it. Otherwise, the tree might not understand and the canoe could split. However, the spruce log for this project had been donated by the logging arm of Sealaska Corporation, the Native regional corporation for Southeast Alaska.

At length Skip Wallen, George's adopted son, who had arranged the project, said to him, "Pop, would it help if we spoke to another canoe tree?" Pop Dalton grabbed right on to that. In Hoonah, he went into the forest with his sons and searched for another canoe tree, one that was straight and free of limbs, sound, and big enough to accommodate a four-fathom canoe such as the one being carved in Glacier Bay. They found a beautiful stout spruce, not far off the road, and the old man talked to the tree. "We are going to hurt you," he explained in Tlingit. "We are going to cut you with sharp instruments because we are going to manufacture an object for survival. We are doing this for a good use, for a noble effort."

Four times the old man walked around the great tree, as was his people's way, paying his respects. A big spruce like that, with a root swell thirty or forty feet in circumference, makes quite a journey for a 90-year-old man with a cane. The moss-coated roots reached to his thighs, thwarting his progress again and again. His sons didn't want him to go around four times. "Once is enough, Pop," they pleaded. But the old man continued slowly around and around on his private errand, and then he felt at peace. The canoe was safe. The wood wouldn't split.

■ *Above:* Art shows, concerts, and theatrical events—both locally performed and on tour from the Lower 48 or abroad—soften the rough edges of wilderness towns. Juneau's Perseverance Theater ranks with the best small theater companies across America. Sitka's annual Summer Music Festival, shown here, has won kudos from such prestigious publications as the *New York Times*.

■ *Above:* Over a hundred years after the Alaska Purchase, the Russian Orthodox faith still burns as brightly as the candles in Sitka's St. Michael's Cathedral. ■ *Right:* Seeking a new supply of valuable sea otter furs, the Russian-American Company moved from Kodiak to Sitka in 1804 and built a settlement guarded with wooden blockhouses, like this replica. ■ *Overleaf:* Like every Southeast community, Sitka (population 8,200) fronts on a busy boat harbor. Seafood processing and a pulp mill drive the economy today.

■ *Left:* The Southeast coast provided a hospitable environment for the original Native inhabitants. The forest gave wood for fuel, shelter, and transportation; materials for weaving, cooking, and storage baskets; and plentiful berries. The sea, ice-free throughout the winter, offered fish, shellfish, and kelp. ■ *Above:* Even the unusual chocolate lily, growing in open, grassy flatlands, provides nourishment. Natives cooked the ricelike pellets of the bulb.

■ *Above:* A power cruiser, favored for salmon fishing and exploring inland waterways, passes the ferry, *MV Aurora*. Smaller ferries sail between "mainline" cities and communities on more distant islands. ■ *Right:* Fall winds howl along Lynn Canal while the massive Chilkat Mountains gather their winter snows. At the head of the seething waterway lie Haines and Skagway, the only northern towns with highway access to interior Alaska and the Lower 48.

■ *Left:* Crew members from the Coast Guard cutter *Planetree* prepare to mount a solar panel. Others pinpoint the ship's position with a sextant. They will replace the buoy within inches of its original location. ■ *Above:* Sitka residents anchor hemlock branches in the water for herring to spawn upon, then harvest the roe, a traditional Native delicacy. ■ *Overleaf:* Seagulls wheel above Icy Strait, near Gustavus, the gateway to Glacier Bay.

These high bush cranberries shielded the leaf from the sun; it failed to develop autumn red.

SOUTHEASTERNERS

My husband and I came to Southeast Alaska because we loved the lush beauty of the forests, mountains, islands, and seas and felt at peace. To us—to many, I think, who find their way to this remote and tranquil coast—Southeast Alaska represented a departure from things we had known too well and didn't like: the freeways and the crowding, the air pollution, the identical lawns and cul de sacs, and the passing by in the street without a wave or a second glance. Moving to Alaska was an act of faith. We had no idea what we would end up doing or how. We knew only that Southeast was where we wanted to be.

Ours is not an uncommon story. Most of the people you meet in Southeast are living exactly where they want to live and doing what they want to do. Alaska is still a place for dreamers. You can still come to this state and try your darndest to do whatever it is you always thought about doing—open a restaurant, produce a play, run a backhoe. For the most part, people aren't going to try and stop you. Unless your dream infringes on somebody else's, people are going to shout "All right!" and thump you on the back, even if they think you're a hopeless fool.

Alaskans exhibit tremendous generosity—generosity of spirit as well as generosity of pocketbook. It's the flat-out acceptance of individuals that strikes me as grand—the toleration of quirks, the forgiveness of foibles and idiosyncrasies. Deep down, we all know we're eccentric to live in such a place as Southeast Alaska, where you can't drive from one town to the next, where moss grows over everything that doesn't move, and where there aren't any snakes or skunks. Sometimes I think Southeasterners are just born feverish. We need the cooling forests and mists to keep us sane.

The generosity of spirit manifests itself in many ways, but in none so much as the way Southeast inhabitants reach out to strangers. Hospitality is widely practiced in Alaska, a remnant of the frontier tradition. In Southeast, people reschedule their days to show visitors around town, then hastily arrange a dinner party and introduce them to the neighbors. I remember receiving a phone call from a friend who had gone to Chicago on business. She had met a man in an elevator who was soon to visit Juneau, and she wanted me to give him the keys to her car so he would have transportation for sightseeing "out the road."

Recently a neighbor and I drove her Honda Civic across Prince of Wales Island, four-wheel-drive pick-up country if ever there was one. Growing fainter of heart with every rocky mile, we decided to buy a second spare tire in the little community of Thorne Bay before tackling the tire-gobbling logging roads on the north end of the island. We pulled up to the garage late in the day to find the mechanics clustered around the doorway, working on a case of Rainier. Discovering without much surprise that none of their tires would fit a Honda, we accepted a beer and sat down to consider. It was then that one of the mechanics turned to another and said, "Hey, your wife drives a Honda!"

"Yeah," the other fellow answered, "but she's in Ketchikan, and so is the car."

"Well, call her up and tell her to put the spare on the morning plane."

At 8:30 the next morning, the scheduled floatplane arrived with our borrowed spare tire, which we returned to Ketchikan (unused, naturally) a few days later.

It is axiomatic that Southeast residents are enthusiastic fishermen and hunters, boaters and skiers, hikers and gatherers. We don't like being cooped up indoors for very long. The people who gravitate toward Southeast Alaska hate to stand in lines, despise filling out forms, rebel at asking permission, and don't care an awful lot what other people think. Southeast was the first place I ever saw a man carrying an infant in front, on his chest, in a Snuglee (a corduroy baby harness). One year we had three house husbands in our small neighborhood up on Starr Hill in Juneau.

At the same time, we are surprisingly cosmopolitan. A person from the tiniest community will likely have traveled to Seattle, and possibly Hawaii, Mexico, or Europe. The acceptance of individuals on their merits attracts a young (thirty-six percent of Alaskans are between the ages of 18 and 34), vigorous, and well-educated population who can readily achieve high-paying, responsible positions. Opportunities abound. When we moved to Juneau in 1971, my husband, fresh out of graduate school, took a job as a research analyst with the Alaska Department of Revenue. It says much about what happens to people in Alaska that only a few months later he was flying over the Canadian Rockies in a chartered Lear jet, whispering numbers into the governor's ear. Artists, photographers, and writers find their creative juices simmering in Southeast. At least a dozen published writers live in Juneau; some forty artists in Haines, a town of eighteen hundred.

You might describe Southeasterners as a collection of independent characters — people like teachers and truckdrivers, totem carvers and accountants, mechanics and musicians — who have given up various comforts in order to live and work in a place of extraordinary beauty and peace. For some, the sacrifice is financial — a twenty-five to thirty percent higher cost of living. For some, it's personal — the distance from family, the break-up of a marriage. Southeast can be hard on marriages. It's not a place that bears unhappiness well.

Some people manage creative compromises to satisfy their diverse needs and longings. An accountant who lives in rural Gustavus, at the entrance to Glacier Bay, works on tax matters in winter and raises strawberries in summer. A designer closes his California office in summer to fly helicopter tours over the Mendenhall Glacier. Another pilot, who is also a professional musician, rises at four in the morning to practice the piano before his day in the air begins.

Everyone who lives in this land of forest and sea gives up the luxury of traveling spontaneously or inexpensively from place to place, and foregoes a lifetime's allotment of sunny weather. For those who choose to stay in this damp and lovely corner of the world, however, the pleasures far outnumber the inconveniences. By and large, people are content.

Eagle and raven, symbols of the two supra-clans in Southeast Native culture, share a lookout.

■ *Left:* A helicopter hovers between water and rainbow in the Ferebee River valley near Skagway. ■ *Above:* Autumn yellows warm the Takshanuk Mountains bordering the Chilkat River near Klukwan. Here colder and drier inland weather produces a hardwood/conifer mix along river valleys, in marked contrast to the impenetrable coastal evergreens. ■ *Overleaf:* The Chilkat Range peaks form a majestic backdrop to historic Fort William H. Seward, in Haines.

■ *Above:* Weathered cannery buildings and derelict fishing boats provide pictur-esque sketch material for artists in Haines (population 1,800). Situated at the northern end of the salmon-rich Lynn Canal, Haines supports a sizable gill net fleet. ■ *Right:* A planked trail crosses a boggy expanse of muskeg. The stunted, twisted trees that endure this acidic habitat can be two hundred years old.

■ *Left:* Glowing with September foliage, black cottonwood trees on the Chilkat River near Haines echo the sawtoothed profile of Mount Emmerich. ■ *Above:* Powerful Chilkat Tlingit Indians controlled the trade passes through the Coast Mountains to the Alaskan and Canadian interior, later used by gold prospectors. Haines was founded by Presbyterian missionary S. Hall Young, who traveled there with naturalist John Muir, discoverer of Glacier Bay.

■ *Above:* Fog conceals the thirty-seven hundred-foot Chilkoot Pass from summer hikers on the thirty-three-mile Chilkoot Trail, which gold-seekers took to the Klondike in 1898. The trail starts in Dyea, nine miles from Skagway. ■ *Right:* A lone cabin stands amid mountain wilderness splendor, an enduring symbol of the Alaska dream. ■ *Overleaf:* Marjorie Glacier, coursing out of the massive Saint Elias Mountains, restlessly strews icebergs into the West Arm of Glacier Bay.

■ *Left:* Workhorses of the precipitous Southeast backcountry, helicopters ferry scientists and explorers into otherwise inaccessible locales. ■ *Above:* Alpine berries display fall foliage on the glacier-scarred landscape of twenty-nine hundred-foot White Pass, which prospectors crossed into the Klondike. The White Pass route was longer but easier than the murderous Chilkoot Trail. Contemporary adventurers cross on the Klondike Highway.

■ *Above:* Belying the minus ten degree Fahrenheit temperature, a lapis sky glows over White Pass on the Klondike Highway, recently visited by a March storm.
■ *Right:* Cushioned hooves allow bewhiskered mountain goats to clamber among rocky outcrops, covered here with winter snow.

■ *Left:* Moose frequent river valleys such as the Chilkat, Taku, and Katzehin, where spring uncurls tender willow leaves. With ample browse, adult males can reach sixteen hundred pounds. ■ *Above:* Sixteen tidewater glaciers converge in the crystalline splendor of Glacier Bay National Park and Preserve. When Vancouver charted Inside Passage waters for Great Britain two hundred years ago, glaciers completely filled the sixty-mile bay.

■ *Above:* Glacial ice absorbs all the colors of the light spectrum except blue, the short wave length. These are reflected back again, accounting for the deep azure appearance of this recently cleaved berg. The denser and deeper the ice, the more intense the color. Surface ice, filled with air pockets, appears white or colorless. ■ *Right:* In May, the sullen ground reluctantly sends forth the showy skunk cabbage, the first flower of a Southeast spring.

Kayakers enjoy the solitude of Riggs Glacier in Glacier Bay.

SEPTEMBER WEEKEND IN ANGOON

The Juneau airport seems strangely subdued as we prepare to take off for Angoon on the west side of Admiralty Island. The summer crowds are gone. In the Bush terminal, a handful of passengers quietly check in for flights to Haines, Pelican, Tenakee Springs, or a half dozen other little burgs scattered across the wilderness. You can pretty much tell a person's business in Alaska by looking at the gear stacked up on the scale. Fishing rods, a big cooler, and an outboard—but no tent—means the party is probably chartering out to one of the one hundred sixty-odd Forest Service cabins in the Tongass National Forest. A tool kit and a box of spare parts means an engine broke down somewhere, and the mechanic is on the way to a fishing boat or wilderness lodge with the means to doctor it back to life. Today, Labor Day eve, deer rifles are much in evidence.

Our Angoon party turns out to be three: Larry and I, and a young Tlingit logger from Hoonah, on the way to visit his girl. A heart-shaped pin on his hat says Evelyn. The pilot asks who wants to sit up front and I don't hesitate an instant before jumping in, even though I know my husband dearly loves the co-pilot's seat, and probably Evelyn's boyfriend does, too. But it's going to be an incredible flight. The lingering overcast has ripped open in billowing clouds that catch on the teeth of the mountains. Selfishly, I want all of this right next to me—the staggering vistas, the sea and islands spreading out beneath us, the cool competence of the pilot, the plane responding to his slightest touch. I want nothing to come between me and the glorious exhilaration of flight.

The pilot climbs in, eases on his headset, flips switches, whispers into a microphone, and we taxi to the runway. The plane, a Cessna 206, is fitted with both pontoons and wheels. Here at the airport we're taking off on wheels, but when we land in Angoon we'll be on floats. We climb above the Mendenhall flats, still dressed in their summer greens, scuttle around the northern tip of Douglas Island, and leapfrog over Stephens Passage to the shaggy mountains of Admiralty. Effortlessly, we coast above muskeg ponds and alpine meadows, drop back to salt water, and follow Chatham Strait south to Angoon. From my co-pilot's seat I can see the new logging roads that cut like whiplashes into the north end of Admiralty, oozing blood of mud and gravel. I can also see whales. Even from this height, I make out their gray-black backs arcing above the sea.

We spot our long, tall friend Bob Grogan even before we land. As we climb from the plane, a blue heron comes to rest in the top of a spruce tree, then kicks off again and flaps away. We load our gear into Bob and Lee's truck and rumble out to the ferry dock. We transfer to the skiff, fire up the Suzuki, and cross the narrow channel to tiny Killisnoo Island, which was a whaling station in the last century. Now, the island amenities consist of an old graveyard, a small fishing lodge, and a few private cabins.

Few man-made objects are as pleasurable as a log cabin in the woods in Alaska. The sweet-smelling logs of a new cabin glow like the yellow of straw. This particular cabin, built from spruce logs cut, peeled, and notched together on the property, faces south down Chatham Strait. The four of us sit before the thermopane window, watching the mountains on Baranof Island, the next big island to the west, darken from pink to lavender-gray. Later on, after we have lighted the oil lamps, a full moon detaches itself from the spruce branches to the left of our view and scribes a low arc in the darkening sky. In the night, the moonlight shines straight into the cabin, waking us. And in the morning, we find tracks leading onto the beach, where the deer danced some mad, moonlit jig.

The mountains disappear with day, obscured by fog. We take our time cooking pancakes on the wood stove, then load the skiff with fishing gear and buckets to replenish the water supply. It's a strange sort of summer in Southeast when the rain can't fill the water buckets. Up past Danger Point, the Angoon handtrollers are doing their slow minuet. We nose into shore where a waterfall bounces down a rock cliff, fill two big plastic containers with frigid water, and then land at Thayer Creek. Pink salmon are still running here, crowding into the deep pockets where the current slackens, and resting before another dash upstream. Not surprisingly, there's a bear track on the bank. When we head for our picnic site, harbor porpoises spot us and rush over like puppies to frolic around the boat.

We are unable to catch a salmon even though every boat around us is hauling them in with typical Native superiority, so we switch to bottom fish gear and concentrate on supper. After ten minutes—too long by Angoon standards—we land two respectable rockfish. There are shelves and halibut holes around Angoon where the local fishermen move off impatiently if they haven't got a fish on in a minute or two, just like there are spots up on these mountain ridges where the deer congregate in herds and invite the hunters to take their pick. Back at the cabin, we fry vegetables and potatoes for rockfish stew and watch for whales from the front deck. On our last morning in Angoon, our luck improves. Lee and Bob bag a good-sized coho, which they'll take back to Juneau and smoke.

We fly out in the early evening. Evelyn has come down to the dock to see her boyfriend off. They stand at a distance from the rest of us, clinging tenderly. We feel a part of their romance now, pleased that the weekend visit has been a success. For the return, our little band has been augmented by a young woman and her shelty, which sits demurely on her lap for the thirty-minute flight. I hang back politely this time. I am content to take the rear seat next to the baggage, alone with my thoughts of homecomings and lovers' partings, of the awful emptiness of leaving and the sweet fulfillment of having been.

As I settle at the window, fishing boats pass beneath my gaze, only to disappear beneath a wisp of cloud. The weather, like fall, is fast closing in. From the looks of the fog draped over Chichagof Island, I don't think you could even get to Tenakee today. But our way is clear enough, back over the mountains and straight into Juneau.

Fall winds and waves batter the fully automated Eldred Rock light station on Lynn Canal.

■ *Left:* Skagway (population 700), staging area for the race to the Klondike in 1898, spills over the Skagway River plain, mountains apart from the gold fields of Canada. A single visiting cruise ship can triple the town's population. ■ *Above:* Restored boomtown shopfronts, part of Klondike Gold Rush National Park, contrast with modern automobiles on Skagway streets. ■ *Overleaf:* Increasing in mass and height as they march northward, the Coast Mountains culminate in 18,008-foot Mount St. Elias, north of Yakutat.

■ *Above:* Advancing or retreating according to climatic changes, glaciers threaten to refigure the surrounding landscape. A case in point: Russell Fiord, near Yakutat, under constant danger of being closed off by surges from Hubbard Glacier (right) and Valerie Glacier (feeding in from left). ■ *Right:* Inviting and cool, the coastal rain forest undergoes a natural cycle of growth and decay.

AFTERWORD

Nowhere else in Alaska, a state known for its stunning vistas, is there more visual richness than in Southeast. From many previous visits, I was well acquainted with this charming scenic region and its friendly, strong people. As I explored the rich forests and meandering seashores, a feeling of deja vu swept over me, a sense of returning to an ancestral land. Among these towering conifers and restless seas, I found my ecological and spiritual home.

Serendipitous experiences are one of the great rewards in the work of a wandering photographer. Without them, the sense of awe, so necessary to my creative juices, is not refueled. Southeast Alaska is the most fascinating area I have explored, and one of the most frustrating to photograph. I had not realized how time consuming travel and logistics would be.

Southeast settlements are spread sparsely throughout the islands and mainland valleys. You can't easily get anywhere else from where you are, and you can't go very far by land once you are there. In Sitka, for example, the road system extends north of town eight miles and south thirteen miles. That's it. Ferries stop five days a week in summer, three in winter. Because I needed my van, I couldn't travel by air.

The light or the view always seemed to be better from the next island, the one out of reach. A rare, fine February day could not be split between Skagway and Haines, just sixteen miles apart, because the next ferry would arrive four days hence—by which time, of course, the weather would have changed. My challenge was to share the visual richness, isolation, and community cohesiveness of life in Alaska's Southeast. Each settlement, set against the rhythms of the sea, has a special personality.

To the people of the Panhandle who opened their hearts and homes and to those who floated and flew me to the farthest reaches of Southeast, my deepest thanks. I wish I could thank each of you personally. Without you this book could not have been possible. On behalf of author Sarah Eppenbach and myself, special thanks to the Alaska Marine Highway System—the ferry crews greeted me so often I began to feel like "family." Thanks also to Alaska Airlines, Alaska Travel Adventures, Eaglecrest Ski Area, Exploration Cruise Lines, Outdoor Alaska, Princess Cruise Lines, Riviera Cruises, Temsco Airlines, Temsco Helicopters, and Todd Harding Charters. Special thanks are also due Juneau photographer Mark Kelley who put me on the other side of the camera for the book jacket, Commander Michael Haucke and the crew of the U.S. Coast Guard cutter *Planetree,* seiner captains Bruce Wallace of the *Sierra Madre* and John Peckham of the *Alsek,* the community of Saxman, and Bishop Gregory and Father Eugene of St. Michael's Cathedral. Thanks, from the author as well, to the employees of the Alaska Department of Fish and Game, the Alaska Division of Parks, the National Park Service, the U.S. Forest Service, and the city visitors centers who patiently answered our many questions.

NANCY SIMMERMAN